Cat-ographies

Ragdolls
Alien Cats

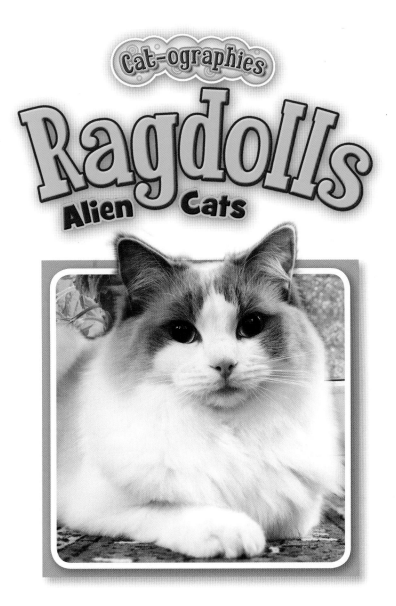

by Judith Bauer Stamper

Consultant: Melissa B. Keefer
Breeder, Pretty Kitty Ragdolls

BEARPORT
PUBLISHING

New York, New York

Credits

Cover and Title Page, © Axel Smidt/Dreamstime; TOC, © Linn Currie/Shutterstock; 4, © AP Images/
Jennifer Szymaszek; 5T, © AP Images/Richard Drew; 5B, © Charles Eshelman/FilmMagic/Getty
Images; 6, Courtesy of Ragdoll Fanciers Club International/rfci.org; 7L, Courtesy of Ragdoll Fanciers
Club International/rfci.org; 7R, © Käfer photo/Shutterstock; 8, © Barbara O'Brien Photography;
9L, © Barbara O'Brien Photography; 9R, © Myotis/Shutterstock; 10T, © Richard Peters/Alamy; 10B,
© Paulette Johnson/Fox Hill Photo; 11, © Yael Tzur/Israel Sun/Landov; 12, © Dave King/ Dorling
Kindersley/Getty Images; 13TL, © Melinda Fawver/Shutterstock; 13TR, © Kendall Saber; 13BL,
© Richard Katris/Chanan Photography; 13BR, © Yves Lanceau/NHPA/Photoshot; 14, © Barbara
O'Brien Photography; 15, © Roberto Della Vite/Marka/Age Fotostock; 16, © Paulette Johnson/Fox
Hill Photo; 17, © Paulette Johnson/Fox Hill Photo; 18, © Barbara O'Brien Photography; 19, © Barbara
O'Brien Photography; 20, © AP Images/Richard Drew; 21, © Axel Smidt/Dreamstime; 22, © R.
Richter/Tierfotoagentur/Alamy; 23, © Linn Currie/Shutterstock.

Publisher: Kenn Goin
Senior Editor: Lisa Wiseman
Creative Director: Spencer Brinker
Design: Dawn Beard Creative
Photo Researcher: Omni-Photo Communications, Inc.

Library of Congress Cataloging-in-Publication Data

Stamper, Judith Bauer.
  Ragdolls : alien cats / by Judith Bauer Stamper.
    p. cm. — (Cat-ographies)
  Includes bibliographical references and index.
  ISBN-13: 978-1-61772-146-5 (library binding)
  ISBN-10: 1-61772-146-8 (library binding)
  1. Ragdoll cat—Juvenile literature. I. Title.
  SF449.R34S73 2011
  636.8'3—dc22
                    2010035158

For more information, write to Bearport Publishing Company, Inc., 101 Fifth Avenue,
Suite 6R, New York, New York 10003. Printed in the United States of America in North
Mankato, Minnesota.

121510
10810CGB

10 9 8 7 6 5 4 3 2 1

Contents

Hotel Cat

When guests arrive at the Algonquin Hotel in New York City, a very special employee named Matilda greets them. Matilda is different from the other staff members. She is a fluffy Ragdoll cat.

Many people stay at the Algonquin because they love seeing Matilda. Each week, she receives many e-mails from fans.

Matilda has been living at the hotel since 1998. She spends her mornings strolling around the hotel's beautiful lobby. When it's time for a catnap, Matilda snoozes on her own little sofa. In the afternoon, Matilda gets to work. She sits by the front desk and greets the guests as they check in, making them feel right at home. Like all Ragdolls, Matilda is a very special kind of cat.

Matilda, shown here on her sofa, is the ninth cat to call the Algonquin home. A cat has been on duty at the hotel since the l930s.

Matilda has a big birthday party every year. Lots of her two-legged and four-legged friends come to the hotel to help her celebrate. At one of her parties, Matilda surprised everyone by jumping right onto the top of the birthday cake. Then she tracked icing all across the hotel lobby.

Matilda celebrating her birthday in 2009

Alien Cats

Unlike other cat **breeds** that got their start hundreds of years ago, Ragdolls were first **bred** in the 1960s. A cat named Josephine, from California, is credited with helping to start the breed.

Where Ragdolls Came From

Josephine lived with her family in Riverside, California.

Some people think that the adult cat in this photo is Josephine. However, most people feel that another cat was used to pose as Josphine.

Josephine's owners noticed that a **litter** of her kittens was different from her earlier ones. Rather than being playful, the kittens were very calm. Their bodies also went **limp**, or flopped, when they were picked up. Ann Baker, a cat breeder, thought they were special. So she bred them, creating the Ragdoll breed. Some people thought Josephine's kittens were different because she had once survived a car accident. They thought the accident had changed Josephine. Baker claimed that the kittens were different because the government had done a **genetic experiment** on Josephine.

Ann holding one of the litters she raised in 1966

Ann Baker also claimed that her Ragdolls represented a **link** between humans and space **aliens**. This is the reason that Ragdolls are often called "alien cats."

Ann Baker bred her Ragdolls to have beautiful, bright blue eyes.

Famous Flop

There is no **evidence** that Ragdolls are a link to aliens or that they were created through government experiments. These are just some of the strange **myths** that surround the breed.

Radolls, however, are unusual in several ways. For example, while most cats are **aloof** and have minds of their own, Ragdolls are **affectionate**, laid-back, and love attention.

Ragdolls love spending time with their owners.

Ragdolls also react in an unusual way when they're picked up—they let their bodies relax and flop down. They look just like a toy rag doll, which is how they got their name. Many people think the cats do this because they are so trusting. However, their tendency to flop is genetic. Breeders select the most **docile** cats to use in their breeding programs.

A rag doll

A young girl holds a Ragdoll kitten that is flopping.

Ragdoll cats are also known for being quiet. They don't meow too often, only when they are trying to tell their owners how they feel about something.

Gentle Giants

Along with their gentle **personalities**, Ragdolls are also known for their big size. They are the second-largest cat breed, topped only by the Maine Coon.

A very large Ragdoll

All Ragdolls have very large heads, big bones, and bushy tails that can be as long as their bodies. Their chest and legs are sturdy and muscular. Their thick hair makes them look even bigger. Female Ragdolls grow up to weigh between 10 and 15 pounds (4.5 and 6.8 kg), while males tip the scales at 15 to 20 pounds (6.8 to 9 kg).

An average pet cat, such as a Siamese (right), weighs between 6 and 10 pounds (2.7 and 4.5 kg). Some Ragdolls are twice as big.

Fabulous Fur

Ragdolls have medium-length hair that is soft, thick, and silky, much like a rabbit's. The cat's hair is also non-matting, which means it doesn't tangle and is easy to care for.

All Ragdolls have light-colored bodies, while their faces, ears, paws, and tails are a darker color. These darker areas are called their points.

tail

ears

face

paws

A Ragdoll's points

There are six different colors that Ragdolls come in: seal point, blue point, chocolate point, lilac point, red point, and cream point. For example, a seal point Ragdoll has points that are the color of dark brown seal fur with a lighter body color.

Ragdolls also come in **patterns** such as **mitted** and **bicolor**.

Seal point Ragdoll

Red point mitted Ragdoll

Chocolate point mitted Ragdoll

Blue point mitted Ragdoll

All these different-colored cats are Ragdolls.

Cutest Kittens

Ragdoll owners think their kittens are the cutest ones around—and for good reason. They are adorable, fluffy balls of fur. When they're born, Ragdoll kittens are all white. Within a week or two, some color starts to show. Their full color, however, doesn't develop until they are two to three years old.

These newborn Ragdoll kittens have soft, white hair.

Though Ragdolls grow up to be big cats, they're extremely little when they're born, weighing between three and four ounces (85 and 113 g).

Ragdoll kittens stay with their mother until they are 12 to 16 weeks old. By that time they're ready to become pets. Many owners like to buy two kittens at a time. This way the kittens have each other to play with, and it's double the fun for the owners.

Ragdoll kittens with their mother

Puppy-Cats

Many owners think their Ragdolls are perfect pets. One reason is that they get along well with children, dogs, and other cats. They also love attention and will follow their owners all over the house, just as a puppy follows its owner around. In fact, Ragdolls are often called "puppy-cats."

This Ragdoll followed its owner into the bathroom and kept her company while she brushed her teeth.

Besides following them around the house, Ragdolls enjoy when their owners hold them like a parent would hold a baby. When being held this way, Ragdolls love to stretch out their front paws and stare up at their owners with their big, blue eyes.

A Ragdoll cat craves attention and affection.

Ragdolls are so easygoing and docile that they won't fight back if attacked by another animal such as a raccoon. For this reason, Ragdolls should always be kept inside or under constant supervision when outdoors.

Cat Tricks

Can you teach a cat tricks? For most cats, the answer is no. For Ragdolls, however, the answer is yes! Ragdolls are very smart, and with a little training, they can be taught to do tricks just like a dog. They can learn to sit, shake paws, and play fetch.

Ragdolls need daily exercise. Since the cats shouldn't go outdoors alone, some owners take their pets out for walks on leashes. Just like a dog, a Ragdoll can be trained to wear a leash and walk around the block with its owner.

Ragdolls also love to climb and play. Some owners buy "cat condos" for their pets. These are little gyms for cats that have several levels for them to exercise, play, and relax on. Ragdolls also like to play with medium-size balls, cardboard boxes, and even paper bags.

A Ragdoll relaxing on its cat condo

Purebred Ragdolls

Many owners enter their Ragdolls in cat shows all over the world. What are some of the things that cat show judges look for? A champion Ragdoll must have beautiful blue eyes, a long bushy tail, silky hair, and the colored points they are known for. Even Matilda, the Ragdoll that lives at the Algonquin Hotel, is a former show cat. In 2006, she was named Cat of the Year at the Westchester Cat show in White Plains, New York.

Matilda received the Cat of the Year honor for all of her charity work. Every year, she raises thousands of dollars at her birthday party, which she gives to animal shelters to help less fortunate cats.

Today, according to **The Cat Fanciers' Association**, Ragdolls are the sixth most popular kind of **purebred** cat. Amazingly, all these purebred Ragdolls have the same **ancestor**—Josephine. Whether a family pet or a show cat, all owners are quick to fall in love with their Ragdolls' gentle personality and wonderful looks.

A Ragdoll

Ragdolls at a Glance

Weight:	Males: 15 to 20 pounds (6.8 to 9 kg); females: 10 to 15 pounds (4.5 to 6.8 kg)
Height:	16 to 18 inches (41 to 46 cm) while sitting
Coat Hair:	Medium to semi-long hair that is plush and silky and doesn't mat
Colors:	Seal point, blue point, chocolate point, lilac point, red point, cream point, as well as various patterns
Country of Origin:	United States
Life Span:	9 to 15 years
Personality:	Very gentle, affectionate, relaxed, and not aggressive
Special Physical Characteristics:	Second-largest cat breed, colored points on coat, tendency to go limp when picked up

Glossary

affectionate (uh-FEK-shuh-nuht) very loving

aliens (AY-lee-uhnz) creatures from another planet

aloof (uh-LOOF) acting distant or not friendly

ancestor (AN-cess-tur) a family member who lived long ago

bicolor (bye-KUHL-ur) having ears, a tail, and a face that is dark colored, though the face has some white hair that's in the shape of an upside-down V; white legs and feet; and a back with lighter-colored patches

bred (BRED) mated cats from specific breeds to produce young with certain characteristics

breeds (BREEDZ) types of cats

Cat Fanciers' Association, The (KAT FAN-see-urz uh-*soh*-see-AY-shuhn, THUH) an organization that keeps records on different cat breeds

docile (DOSS-uhl) calm and easy to train or control

evidence (EV-uh-duhnss) information that helps prove that something is true

experiment (ek-SPER-uh-ment) a scientific test set up to find the answer to a question

genetic (juh-NET-ik) having to do with the way that a person or animal's physical and mental characteristics are passed from one generation to another through genes

limp (LIMP) floppy and not firm

link (LINGK) a connection between things or people

litter (LIT-ur) a group of baby animals born to the same mother at the same time

mitted (MIT-id) having a face, a tail, legs, and ears that are dark colored; a lighter-colored body; and a white chin, paws, and chest

myths (MITHS) stories that often tell of larger-than-life beings and mysterious events

patterns (PAT-urnz) a repeating arrangement of colors and shapes

personalities (*pur*-suh-*NAL*-uh-teez) the combination of qualities or traits that make one person or animal different from others

purebred (PYOOR-bred) an animal whose parents, grandparents, and other ancestors are all the same kind of animal

23

Index

Bibliography

Alderton, David. *Cats (Smithsonian Handbook).* New York: Dorling Kindersley (2002).

Davis, Karen Leigh. *Ragdoll Cats: (Complete Pet Owner's Manual).* Hauppauge, NY: Barron's (1999).

Fields-Babineau, Miriam. *Cat Training in 10 Minutes.* Neptune City, NJ: T.F.H. Publications (2003).

Read More

Miller, Connie Colwell, and Gail Saunders-Smith. *Ragdoll Cats (Pebble Books).* Mankato, MN: Capstone Press (2008).

Stone, Lynn M. *Ragdoll Cats (Eye to Eye with Cats).* Vero Beach, FL: Rourke Publishing (2010).

Strobel, Gary, and Susan A. Nelson. *Guide to Owning a Ragdoll Cat.* Neptune City, NJ: T.F.H. Publications (2002).

Learn More Online

To learn more about Ragdoll cats, visit
www.bearportpublishing.com/Cat-ographies

About the Author

Judith Bauer Stamper has written both fiction and nonfiction books about animals. She lives with her cat in New Jersey, near New York City.